INTRODUCTION

Fermented or cultured foods have quite a long history across the globe and has been known to thrive in all sorts of native diets. For years, people have been using fermentation as a way to increase their overall health and well being. The process of fermentation or culturing helps to produce what are known as beneficial microbes. These microbes are very important for overall

human health as they work to create a balance within your intestines and your intestinal flora. When the right balance is in place, you are then working to boost your immunity and more.

To go even further, your stomach actually works as a second brain and can produce more and more of the vital neurotransmitter known as serotonin, which has a great impact on your mood. A healthy gut will in turn make it so that you have a healthier mind and body as well.

Taking a look at fermented foods, these items are known for being some of the best items for natural detoxification and chelation. This means that they have the ability to help your body to rid itself of a range of toxins, including some of the heavy metals that we accumulate in our system over time. People who start to introduce fermented foods, especially vegetables, into their diets are able to work on their very own detoxification system. These incredible food items are key when it comes to self-healing, and you do not even have to consume them in large quantities to get the full benefit.

Depending on the types of cultured or fermented foods that you have on hand at any given time, you can add around 1/4 to 1/2 cup to your meals up to three times a day. If you are new to fermented foods and veggies, you may start to notice that you are going to start to develop a range of detox symptoms that are also known as the healing crisis if you start to take on too many of these foods at one time. As you start out, you can introduce certain items to your daily diet in smaller servings and then work your way up to other foods as you go along. This gradual increase will help your microbiota within your intestines to have the time that is necessary to fully adjust instead of coming on as more of a shock to your system.

TYPES OF FERMENTED FOODS

In addition to your traditional fermented fruits and vegetables, you will also find that there are a number of different items, including beverages that you can add to your diet. Each of the foods will work with your stomach to help you promote a healthy balance and overall good well being. Just some of the fermented foods that you can make yourself at home include, but are not limited to:

- Chutney
- Cultured Vegetables, including a range of baby food purees
- Condiments such as mayonnaise and salsa
- Fish varieties to include gravlax and mackerel
- Cultured Dairy, including sour cream, kefir and various yogurts

While you can still get some great benefits from taking supplements and probiotics, there is a whole lot more that fermented foods such as vegetables can give you to help you keep the balance of intestine bacteria on point. The lactic acid yeast involved in the fermentation process is there to promote the growth of the good bacteria found within the intestines. Fermented and cultured foods are naturally rich in a lot of the different minerals, vitamins and enzymes that our bodies need. Not only are they like having a power pack for your insides, but they are also able to help promote and maintain incredible digestive health that will in turn make you feel wonderful.

EASY STEPS TO MAKE FERMENTED VEGETABLES AT HOME

The wonderful thing about fermented vegetables is that you have an amazing selection to choose from. If you are able to pick out vegetables that are in season, you are going to be able to also save a whole lot of money and stretch out your food budget. Today, there are many people who are taking back control of their bodies by making sure that they have a digestive system that is fully in balance. This is one series of steps that you can use when you are ready to start making some of your own fermented vegetables at home:

1. Look for variety. By taking a look at the vegetables that are available to you in any given season, you can pick and choose some of your favorites to get started. Some of the best choices to give you a great variety will include organic veggies such as peppers, carrots, collard greens, kale, seaweed and broccoli. As you go on, you are going to be able to put together a list of some of your favorite vegetables to work with while introducing some new options to keep the variety and menu fresh.

2. Work with a brine that will help you to easily ferment your vegetables. The most popular brine is done by using the juices from stalks of celery. A wonderful vegetable, celery has a good level of natural sodium that has the ability to keep all of the veggies that you are fermenting in an environment that is anaerobic in nature. This is the best way to encourage the growth of healthy bacteria during the fermentation process.

3.   Once you have a good brine, you can then place your vegetables into it by way of a jam jar or canning jar. During this step, you will want to be sure that you fill the jar to the brim so that you are eliminating any trapped air from ruining the process. Depending on what you like and the type of recipe that you are going to be using, this is the time where you can also add in some of your favorite aromatics including rosemary or garlic to help enhance the taste. After this step is finished, you will want to cover over the mixture completely with a cabbage leaf.

4.   Upon placing a proper seal on the jar, you will need to be sure that you keep it for anywhere from two to four days in an area that is slightly moist and warm. Some seasoned veggie fermenters will use a type of portable cooler that they will fill with warm water to help them store any of the jars that they have filled. Another useful option is simply covering over the jars with wet, warm towels and the setting them in some sort of a casserole dish that you can then fill with warm water. It is important that you make sure that the temperature range is able to stay between 68 and 75 degrees Fahrenheit to get the best possible result.

5.   After you have let the jars sit and ferment for the days desired, you can move them into a refrigeration unit for proper storage until you are ready to consume them. You are going to find that simply chopping up your favorite vegetables into bite size pieces and fermenting them will make for an incredible addition to salsa, as a garnish and of course, for a delicious side dish.

WHAT IS LACTO-FERMENTATION?

Lacto-fermentation is a method in which you preserve foods while also enhancing the overall nutrient content to be found within. This action that takes place with the bacteria works to make the minerals found in cultured foods more plentiful and readily available within the human body. This same bacteria is also able to produce valuable B vitamins as well as enzymes that are very beneficial when it comes to healthy digestion.

You will find that just about any type of vegetable is able to be fermented by using any number of simple techniques. Farm fresh and organic produce is the absolute best way to help provide amazing nutrition in the form of fermented foods that will be usable all year long. You can work by fermenting one vegetable by itself or you can put together your own mix or follow a recipe to come up with any sort of combination. The different herbs and spices that you can add, otherwise known as the aromatics, can truly enhance the flavors and give you a better variety of cultured foods.

GETTING STARTED - EQUIPMENT

You are going to find as you get started that the right equipment can make a world of difference. This equipment can include everything from your favorite knives for cutting and chopping to the perfect vessel to be used in the fermentation process. The bottom line is that you will want to be sure that you have all of the right equipment on hand to suit your needs so that you do not find yourself in the middle of the preparation process without enough to work with. Some of the items that you could choose from as you work to ferment your favorite veggies could include:

- Chopping Tools, such as a knife set, food processor or a mandolin slicer
- Cutting board
- Potato masher, which can be used for certain vegetables so that you can get the juices out
- Containers to hold vegetables or hold them for pounding out the juices
- Pickling salt or unrefined sea salt
- Choice of starter cultures, which can include kefir grains, whey, freeze dried starters and more
- Filtered water to help wash the vegetables
- Fermentation vessels

CHOOSING YOUR FERMENTATION VESSELS

There are really countless options when it comes to picking out the types of containers that you would like to use to ferment your veggies, fruits and condiments. The best vessels will range from ceramic crocks to glass jars with a widened mouth opening. You will find, however, that a basic cylindrical shape is what is recommended as it helps the fermentation process along more than a container that has hard, sharp corners.

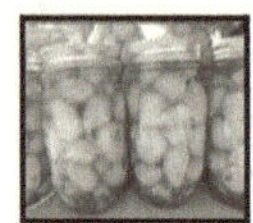 Glass or ceramic is most recommended, however you can use plastic as long as you keep in mind that the plastic can actually leach chemicals, is much more prone to scratches and can even hold in harmful bacteria. If a plastic container is all that you have on hand, you need to make sure that it is completely made from food grade plastic and that it has not been used in the past for holding any sort of non-food items. You should never ferment foods in metal containers as they will react almost immediately with both the salt as well as the acids that are produced as fermentation takes place.

Here are just a few of the different types of fermentation vessels that you can use:

- **Canning Jars Or Glass Jars** - Glass canning jars are relatively inexpensive and you can find them in a number of stores or even in bulk online. You can get the glass jars in a wide variety of sizes so that you also have options when it comes to making a half batch or even for your salsas, chutneys or condiments.

- **Ceramic Crocks** - You can usually find a variety of ceramic crocks online, at estate sales and even thrift stores in your local area. Not only are they wonderful for decoration when not in use, but they are also quite practical for the fermentation process. Simply take the time to make sure that your ceramic crock is free of lead, where it will usually be stamped as containing lead-free clay. When you choose ceramic crocks as your fermentation vessels, you will also want to make sure that there are not any cracks that can also keep the harmful bacteria inside.

- **Slow Cooker Inserts** - You may find that you have a slow cooker not being used, in which case you can use the ceramic insert. If not, you may be able to find them for sale in one of your local stores. No matter where you get them, these ceramic inserts are wonderful for fermentation. In this case, either a round or oval insert can be used.

- **Ceramic Or Glass Bowls** - Both options in either ceramic or glass bowls are a great option when you are looking to start fermenting your own foods. The chances are very good that you already have some right in your cabinets in a variety of sizes.

- **Ceramic Fermenting Crock** - This is an all in one option that will come complete with everything that you need for fermentation in terms of a vessel. These crocks will come with the pot itself, the lid and even internal stones for weight that will keep the veggies perfectly submerged beneath your brine. The lids themselves are designed with a special air lock system that will allow natural gases to escape while also keeping out the oxygen. This helps to drastically reduce or even eliminate the threat that mold can grow while the culturing process is taking place. These all in one crocks will come in different sizes, so you can take the time to decide what is best for your family's needs. While these specialty crocks can be more expensive, they are generally the best type of vessel that you can have for the fermentation process.

- **Glass Jars Complete With Air Lock Systems** - A great alternative to the specialty crocks, glass jars can come equipped with an air locking system and are actually less expensive. The air lock system works just like the ceramic fermenting crocks and they come in a wide variety of sizes. You may not find that a weight will be necessary for this option, however you may want to use one to help make sure ether the top layer of the veggies do not dry out or turn color.

COVERING AND WEIGHTING METHODS

If you do not have a vessel that comes complete with its own weight system, you will need to make sure that you are able to find one that is gig to suit your needs. The method that will work best will generally depend on the kinds of foods that you are fermenting and the actual vessel itself.

Non-Brined Veggies, Fruits and Condiments - When you are working with foods that are not going to be using a brine, the recipe may simply call for a lid to be placed on top of the container so that the food inside can ferment for a few days. Because small levels of gas will be produced during the fermentation period, it is always best that the lid is removed with caution.

Veggies In Brine - In the case of working with vegetables using a brine, you will want to go with a weight and cover system. After you have filled your vessel with the veggies and then covered them with brine, the weighting mechanism will need to fit inside. Vegetables that are left in a brine will start to float up to the top as the fermentation process progresses. Any exposure to the open air will cause mold to grow so you need to make sure that they are able to remain submerged at all times to help keep them protected.

WEIGHTING OPTIONS

If you are able to find a plate that is able to fit nice and snug inside the vessel, you may be able to have a good amount of luck. Additionally, you can place a clean rock or another object in similar heft on top of the plate to keep it down and the veggies submerged. You can also try the following things to weight it down, just remember that everything must be completely cleaned first:

- A heavy ceramic or glass coaster
- Smaller jars that will fit inside the vessel filled with water
- Other objects can be used for weighting just as long as they are free from chemicals, glues and they are completely clean

After the vegetables are weighted properly, you may want to be sure that you cover the top of your chosen vessel with some sort of lid, coffee filter, plastic or even a tightly woven cloth that will keep any potential bugs out and the odors inside. If using towels, you will need to be sure that you secure them tightly with a rubber band. Because the fermentation process creates gases that will need to escape, you have to be sure that you are usage a covering that will allow them to escape easily. At the same time, it is crucial that you keep oxygen getting inside to a minimum. The more oxygen that you allow in, the greater your chances will be of developing mold and scum that can and will ruin your efforts.

If you decide to go without a cover and a weighting system, you can take the initiative to submerge your vegetables daily, by hand. In this case, you will start to notice that a white film will begin to develop along the surface. You will need to scrape it off each day as this is an accumulation of yeast bodies so if it gets into your batch it is not going to be harmful for consumption purposes.

PREPARING YOUR VEGETABLES FOR FERMENTATION

As you start in on your journey to ferment your favorite vegetables, you will need to learn more about the best methods of preparation. This may mean looking at a number of different recipes until you find preparation methods that you like best or simply trying out new things from time to time. Believe it or not, there are many people who will go back and forth on the correct way to cut up the vegetables.

The way in which you prepare your veggies will start to have an impact on the outcome of your fermented product. In some cases, you may even notice that other ingredients may need to be added to certain cutting methods to help create the best possible finished product. Of course, you have the option of chopping, slicing or grating all of your favorite vegetables, so the choice is ultimately personal preference.

CHOPPING

 A vegetable that has been chopped is simply cut into small pieces that are relatively bite sized. A good reference point is that chopped vegetables will usually mean having the ability to fit several bits in each bite of food that you take. As you chop up a vegetable for fermentation, you can make it that small or even opt for larger bites. With most recipes, you can go for a chop that is about an inch in size or a bit smaller. Vegetables that are chopped will usually require some sort of a brine of water and salt.

One of the biggest things that you will need to take into consideration in terms of size to use for chopping your veggies is the overall length of time that it will take for them to fully culture. A carrot stick that is hard will usually take twice the amount of time that grated carrot will as the brine will have to work to penetrate the carrot stick. Depending on their size, chopped vegetables can take a lot longer than thinly sliced vegetables or those that have been grated.

It goes without saying that the actual method of chopping requires much less time when compared to slicing or grating the vegetables. You can rough chop some of the chunks of your favorite vegetables and then toss them in with your favorite fermentation recipes. Some of the best candidates for chopping will include veggies such as:

- Cucumbers
- Zucchini
- Peppers
- Summer Squash
- Eggplant
- Carrots
- Green Beans
- Asparagus

SLICING

Thinly slicing your vegetables is very similar to grating because it allows for the entire surface area of the veggie to be completely covered with the brine. Thinly sliced vegetables like with sauerkraut that are long will usually create their own brine.

However, other vegetables will have a cellular structure that will need a brine for the best possible result. Even though you will have the ability to toss together some cabbage that has been thinly sliced and the appropriate seasonings to make sauerkraut, you will find that a thicker slice of cucumber will have to have a brine in order to properly culture and help maintain a deceit crunch. Some of the best choices for slicing include:

- Cucumber
- Peppers
- Celery
- Cabbage
- Zucchini
- Summer Squash

A lot of the recipes that you will find will call for either chopping or grating of the vegetable for fermentation. It is important that you take into consideration the composition of the vegetable so that you can decide whether or not it will be smarter to use a brine or to go without.

Vegetables that are sliced are usually in the middle when it comes to culturing times. You may have a wider window to work with if you find that you need to be able to move your fermenting veggies into a refrigerate unit if you are going to be leaving down or you find that you leave it culturing for too many days in a row.

GRATING

If you are planning on grating your vegetables, you have the option of either doing it by using a box grater or putting the veggies into a food processor. Most of the crunchier, harder vegetables will often call for grating in the majority of recipes that are out there. Choices for grating will include veggies such as:

- Cabbage
- Carrots
- Turnips
- Cucumber
- Zucchini
- Radish
- Beets

Out of all of the preparation techniques, grating vegetables for fermentation will create a larger surface area. The more surface area you have, the more salt will be able to penetrate the vegetables. This will lead to moisture being

drawn out much quicker and it actually works to create its own brine. Whenever you grate your vegetables you are basically preparing a cultured vegetable that self-brines. These veggies will usually come out with a texture similar to a relish once they are finished.

There are a lot of people that will make sauerkraut by grating up their cabbage by using a food processor. While this is a quick way to make it so that the brine is produced, it isn't always necessary to achieve a sauerkraut that is self-brining. Overall, the grated veggies are usually the quickest when it comes to being cultured because of the increase in surface area.

TIPS FOR DELICIOUS FERMENTED VEGETABLES

The more that you get involved with fermentation and cultured foods, the more you will learn about your favorite ways to prepare each vegetable. To get started, there are some helpful tips that you can keep in mind that will give you a solid basis for fermenting your own vegetables quickly and easily. Just remember to get the best results, always use vegetables that are fresh and organic.

You will find that roughly five or six medium heads of cabbage will give you around 32 ounces or 10 to 14 jars of fermented veggies of quart size.

It is a good rule of thumb to make sure that cabbage makes up around 80% of your overall vegetable blend. You will see that sweet potatoes, beets, carrots, turnips and many other veggies of the hard root variety will make for an incredible base for your fermented veggies. Because they are not always as economical as other vegetables, it is best to look for them when they are in season.

In some cases, you may find that the skins of your vegetables can add a bitter taste so you can always peel them before slicing, chopping or grating.

While you work on different recipes, never be afraid to add some different vegetables to fit in with your tastes. Using orange, yellow or red bell peppers, dill, kale, parsley, different color beets, butternut squash, or collard greens will give you a twist on traditional options. However, if you are going to be using bell peppers, it is good to remember that they can give a rather strong presence after fermentation takes place. Use sparingly as one smaller pepper is going to be just right for between 12 and 14 jars.

Either green or red cabbage can be used in your mix, however you will need to make sure that they are healthy and dense with a hard and heavy feel to them. The leafier versions of cabbage do not ferment as well and they tend to turn to mush in most cases.

Onion can actually overpower your mixture, even if you are taking care to only use a little bit. Of course, you are going by your tastes so if you like them, you can use them sparingly with your other vegetables.

Any sort of aromatic, including onions, ginger and garlic will actual increase in flavor quite a bit while they ferment, so you will usually want to experiment with how much you should be using. A little can go a long way so you never want to overdo it in any way. For example, two or three medium sized cloves of garlic can be just what you need to give around a dozen jars a mild garlic flavor.

If you are going to be adding herbs, it is important that you only use those that are fresh and organic in smaller amounts. Some of the different herbs that are great with fermentation include thyme, basil, sage, oregano and rosemary to name a few.

When it comes to starter cultures you can use two packets for any batch that you will be making for around 12 to 14 jars during the summer season. If you are making a batch during the winter months, you are going to find that three packets will yield a better final result.

In the summer, you will generally find that your vegetables will be done between three and four days. For the winter fermentation process, you may need around seven days for the best result. By simply opening up the jar and having a taste, you will be able to tell when they are ready to your liking. Once they are done, all you have to do is simply move the jars into your refrigerator.

Seaweed and sea veggies can be added to your mixture to help you increase the fiber content as well as the level of minerals and vitamins inside. Whole dulse or flakes can be tossed in as well as sea palm and wake. These two do not have a fishy flavor and they will need to be diced after you presoak them. If you want to add a fishier flavor, you can look for hijack or arame to add to your vegetable mixture.

BRINES, SALTS AND STARTERS

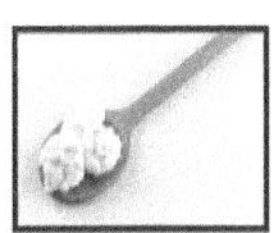 You may find that there will be different recipes that may specifically call for salt, a starter culture or even a combination of both salt and whey. Some of the most common starter cultures used with those that ferment vegetables will include Body Ecology or Caldwell. The method that is used will vary between recipes and you can even adjust them to suit your own personal tastes as well as any restrictions that you may have on your diet. In some situations, you can adjust the starter that is used or the amount of salt depending on the types of vegetables that you want to use.

Starter cultures such as kefir grains, whey, freeze dried cultures and even, salt can help to promote a quality fermentation process. These items all work to inhibit the growth of microorganisms that are less than desirable and they promote the growth of beneficial lactobacilli. In some situations, you will even find that they can add to the beneficial bacteria needed in the culturing process. The combination that you choose to go with will usually depend on the project at hand and any sort of dietary restrictions that you or anyone in your family has.

The skins of your fruits and vegetables will usually contain a level of natural bacteria that is picked up during both the farming process and then through transportation. If allowed to grow, this bacteria will start to ferment your produce.

Not all of the bacteria present are created equally and there are some that will start to impact the taste of your finished product. The addition of salt or other additives will help to inhibit the growth of these undesirable microorganisms while helping to promote the good bacteria strains that you are looking for. In general, a natural culturing process is able to get encouraged and sped up with the introduction of starter cultures, kefir grains, whey and more. Most of the recipes that you will find will encourage the use of salt or other starter cultures, however they are not always necessary and you can adjust them according to your own personal tastes.

SALT

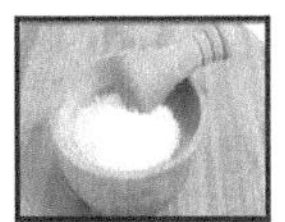

Throughout history, salt has always been used as a way to preserve foods and keep them good when there was no means for refrigeration. Vegetables will always ferment a lot better when they are under the protection of salt after it has been dissolved in water or a brine. The salt will work to pull out any moisture that is in the food, thus denying bacteria that perfect living conditions that they need to live and then grow, with the exception of course of the Lactobacilli strains that are tolerant to salt.

The salt works to suppress the growth of mold and bacteria and it lends to a much slower process of fermentation that is just right for vegetables that will need to be stored for a longer period of time. If you decide to use salt without any sort of starter, you are actually allowing the natural bacteria on the vegetables to take care of the fermentation process for you.

Salt is known for hardening the pectin found in vegetables that will leave them crunchy while also working to enhance the flavors overall. When you use more salt, the saltier the taste and the slower the fermentation process will be. Unfortunately for many people who are new to fermentation, adding too much salt is very easy to do. This is why it is mostly recommended to salt only to taste unless you have a need for storing for a longer period of time. Depending on what you are fermenting, more salt will usually be used with sauerkraut and pickles while less is usually put in when it comes to fruits, mayonnaise and ketchup.

If you are using a preparation that has less salt, you will see that it will not only ferment a lot faster but you will also be likely to see the white film that is known to develop along the surface. This film, which is an accumulation of yeast bodies, is easy to scrape off. However, you should know that it is not harmful in any way so it is alright if some of it gets into your batch of fermented vegetables. The salt free ferments can result in mushy vegetables as they are bio-diverse in nature. If you want to use a salt free ferment, you can always substitute with seaweed or celery juice, however you still could end up with the mushier texture.

STARTER CULTURES

If you use some type of bacterial starter with your fermentation process can speed things up for you. There are a number of starters that you can try, and in most cases you will start to develop your favorites. Because the type of starter used can have a direct impact on the taste of the fished product, it is always best to try out a few different kinds until you find one that you really like.

Kefir Grains - Milk or water kefir grains can be added in with your vegetable ferment mixes. All you have to do is take them and mix them in with your desired vegetables and then once they are fermented, you can actually eat the grains or fish them out depending on your taste. After you have used wither your water kefir grains or milk kefir grains in a vegetable fermentation, you will not be able to use them again in some sort of sugar or milk based beverage. It is always recommended that new grains are used in each batch of fermented vegetables that you will be making. Salt is always optional in these ferments and it can slow down, yet enhance the flavor and keep the crunch while still helping to protect from the development of mold.

Whey - If you are lactose intolerant, you will not want to use whey as it is dairy based. The whey infuses the veggies with the good bacteria that you want and it common for use with a wide variety of fermentation recipes. Making sure that the whey that you use is strained properly and also fresh tasting will add a whole lot of good flavor to the batch. You can also add salt along with the whey if you choose to add flavor and it can also keep the veggies nice and crunchy. The use of whey without salt will speed up the process but you could end up with the dreaded mushy texture. Whey can be made by simply straining kefir, buttermilk or yogurt.

DRIED CULTURES

Starter cultures are basically dried bacteria that is packaged in foil that you can mix into your fermentation vessel. The culture can be stored in your freezer and you can simply take them out as you need to use them. When used, this is a nice and easy way to quickly speed up the fermentation process. A starter culture is basically a known set of bacteria that you are adding in. It is not always necessary to buy a dried culture but you will usually find that the results will be much more consistent in nature. You will also see that dried starter cultures are paired well with salt for a good taste along with crunch and mold protection.

A lot of the vegetable starter cultures that you will find will include dairy as a sort of carrier agent for the culture itself. There are certain brands that if you use them in the measurements indicated on the instructions, the levels of dairy to be found in the finished product is usually so small that they are basically below trace amounts.

BATCH TRANSFER JUICES

Once you have already made a batch of great tasting fermented vegetables, you can actually use a few tablespoons of the juice in the container to add to a new batch. This is a wonderful way to carry over the starter and it comes in quite handy, especially when you are someone who is always making fermented veggies. Of course, you will still want to add salt to taste if you want to have mold protection along with a great texture that is nice and crunchy.

SUBSTITUTIONS IN FERMENTATION RECIPES

There may come a time when you find yourself using a recipe and you are out of a particular ingredient that is called for or you would actually prefer to use another ingredient intend. Each recipe is different and you will see that your taste may be different than the next person. With that being said, these are some great substitutions that are good to have on hand should you ever feel the need to switch things up a bit:

Salt substitutions - Using a salt free ferment can actually lead to mushy veggies even though they are much more bio-diverse. If you are looking for a salt free ferment, you can go with seaweed or even celery juice, yet you will not be able to get any sort of a crunchy texture.

Whey substitutions - There are a lot of recipes that will call for whey as a starter, however you actually have several great options for a substitution. In some cases, you will be able to go with more salt in the recipe instead of fully replacing the whey with some sort of starter culture. Another good option is go with a starter culture like kefir grains, with water kefir grains being used in the place of milk kefir grains if you need to recipe to be dairy free.

A freeze dried culture can be used as well or even the juice from another batch of vegetables that you just finished up as long as it was a successful and good tasting one. For a freeze dried culture, you simply follow the instructions that came along with the culture to figure out how much of the packet you will need to use when taking the amount of vegetables into consideration. If you are using a packet that is said to culture around 4 or 5 pounds, you might be able to use less of it if you have a recipe that is for 2 pounds. When using juice as a substitute, you will need to be sure that you have at least the same amount that was called for with whey in the recipe or even more if you have it available.

Dried starter culture substitutions - Whenever you have a recipe that asks for any type of pre-packaged culture as a starter, you can usually simply substitute it with salt or even a combination of both salt and another alternative culture such as kefir grains, whey or leftover juice from a previous vegetable batch. Each quart of fermented vegetables will need around 1 to 3 teaspoons of salt and about 1/4 of whey or 1/4-1/2 cup of juices from another batch to be successful.

A lot of your recipes for fermented vegetables will be salt friendly so adding a bit of salt in place of a dried culture or whey will not normally ruin the taste. Some items such as condiments, fruits, salsa and dips can end up being more sensitive to salt so it is usually best to skink with a dried culture, whey or kefir grains instead of simply reaching for extra salt.

FERMENTED FOOD OPTIONS AND RECIPE IDEAS

No matter what type of economy we are living in, there are always people looking to help save some money. Fermented foods are not only a perfect way to help cut down on the grocery bill but they are wonderful choices to help provide your family with healthy options that will aid indigestion. Making your own fermented items at home is easier than you may think and you can actually save anywhere from 25% up to 95% whenever you go to the grocery store, especially if you go with fruits and vegetables that are in season and affordable.

Yogurt - Hands down one of the most popular cultured food item, yogurt is found in most households across the globe. While this is a delicious food

item, it can end up being rather costly, especially if you are going for some of the organic varieties if you even have them available in your local store.

Organic yogurt options will cost around $3.59 in a quart size while a conventional brand will be around $2.29 per quart. If you make your own using organic ingredients, you will be spending around $1.25 a quart for a 65% savings and with conventional ingredients it will cost you around $.75 per quart for a nice savings of around 67%. Overall, it takes about 15 minutes to prepare your own yogurt and between 6 to 24 hours to fully culture.

Sauerkraut - Even if you look hard for raw and unpasteurized sauerkraut in your local grocery store complete with live cultures, the chances are that you may not find it. If you do happen to find it, you will usually see that it will be very expensive to buy. You can actually save around 50% when you take the time to make it yourself at home. The best part is that you can add your own flavor enhancements to make sure that you have a perfect mix, including anything from shredded apple or dried juniper berries.

You can also take some other vegetables and shred them up such as carrots to really bring out a new flavor and add some depth to the texture. When you are able to buy cabbage and some of your other vegetables in season, you are able to enjoy even more savings. From the store, sauerkraut of good quality is going to cost you around $7.67. Made at home from organic ingredients, you are looking at a cost of around $4.20 for a 45% savings. When using conventional ingredients, you can make it for around $2.36 with a savings of around 69%. The prep time is around 20 minutes and then it can take about a week to 10 days to culture fully.

HEALTH BENEFITS OF FERMENTED VEGETABLES

There are all sort of studies that are now showing just how beneficial fermented foods can be for not only our digestion processes but also for our overall health. Taking in fermented foods such as yogurt each day will help to boost health and even promote longevity. There are a lot of people that are now understanding just how important probiotics are for our bodies, especially when you take into consideration all of the processed foods that people are consuming today.

There are many people who are not getting the right amount of good bacteria in their system so it is always good to look for fermenting as a way to bring some of the quality bacteria back into the body. Not only is fermenting vegetables a fun process that is rewarding but it can also be a whole lot cheaper than buying goods pre-made.

Detoxification - The microbes that you are able to consume when you eat fermented vegetables are wonderful when it comes to detoxifying. For many years, vegetables have been fermented to help preserve them and keep them from spoiling. A lot of the pickled products that you will find in your local grocery store today have been fermented, such as pickles, ketchup and sauerkraut. Each of these items have the ability to purify and help detoxify on some level when consumed. The process of detoxification is a great way to help eliminate a lot of the toxins that can be found in the broth, including various heavy metals that are known to accumulate over time.

Infection Defense - There can be a whole lot of competition between microbes within the body. Good bacterial will work to fight off any of the foreign matter that will enter into the intestinal tract. This good bacteria actually acts as a first line of defense when it comes to fighting infections of all sorts. There are different substances that are produced by lactic acid bacteria, or lactobacilli, that are known to inhibit some of the more harmful organisms. Lactobacillus acidophilus helps to make several substances that are known to protect human cells and fight off pathogenic bacteria such as salmonella.

Nutritious and Delicious - Fermented veggies and other products are wonderful in terms of the amount of amino acids, minerals and vitamins that they contain. Fermentation actually works to boost the levels of vitamins in some cases and fermented milk is well known for being full of B vitamins. If you are fermenting vegetables at home, you are actually giving yourself a higher concentration of vitamin C, which has long been known as being very beneficial to health.

Fermented foods, especially vegetables, are loaded with all sorts of probiotics or beneficial microbes that work hard to keep the digestive tract in perfect working order. In addition to that, these microbes are wonderful for heart health, to boost immunity, cut down on various food allergies and even lessen the risk of obesity and diabetes.

The large amount of good bacteria to be found in fermented vegetables is quite staggering, making it easier to see that they will be able to fully survive a trip all the way throughout the digestive tract. Fermented foods such as veggies, sauerkraut, yogurt and kefir are really some of the top super foods. Whenever you are hoping to bring a whole new level of goodness to your body to bring your overall health up and promote well being, you are going to find that there is nothing tastier and easier to make and eat than fermented vegetables.

If you happen to be someone who has digestive problems, the last thing that you may want to reach for is a supplement or any kind of medication. In order to work on this sort of an issue, you will need to be able to help bring back the natural balance that your body needs in terms of the disease causing bacteria and the beneficial bacteria that is naturally located in your digestive system. Fermented foods, or those that are high in beneficial bacteria, is the perfect way to get the right amount of good stuff back into your body to help you restore the much needed balance.

Traditional fermented vegetables and other foods are just loaded with lactic acid bacteria, which are the organisms that are responsible for the actual process of fermentation. The lactic acid bacteria helps the milk to get sour for sour cream or yogurt and it will help to ferment vegetables for side dishes, added ingredients and much more. You are going to find that learning how to make fermented veggies at home will not only be a fun process but also one that is very rewarding and affordable, especially when you take all of the health benefits into account.

With the benefits of self-healing and natural detoxification, it's no wonder that many more people are beginning to ferment their own vegetables. Using this guide can get your intestinal system balanced and clean out many of the toxins that end up attacking other parts of your body.

You can boost your immunity and improve your mental health as your stomach begins producing more serotonin and less toxins. Start your journey to good health today!